When this wonderful little book by Warren Bluhm first dropped into my hands a decade ago, I thought it was important. Today, I think it's particularly vital.

— Wally Conger

Books by Warren Bluhm
Full
24 flashes
Gladness is Infectious
How to Play a Blue Guitar
A Bridge at Crossroads
Refuse to be Afraid
Refuse to be Afraid: 10th Anniversary Edition
A Scream of Consciousness
Myke Phoenix: The Complete Novelettes
The Imaginary Revolution
The Imaginary Bomb

The Roger Mifflin Collection
The Haunted Bookshop – Christopher Morley
Men in War – Andreas Latzko
Trivia – Logan Piersall Smith
The Man Who Was Thursday – G.K. Chesterton
The Demi-Gods – James Stephens
War Poems – Siegfried Sassoon
And more to come ...

Also edited by Warren Bluhm
Resistance to Civil Government – Henry David Thoreau
Letters to the Citizens of the United States – Thomas Paine
A Book of Secrets

WarrenBluhm.com

Refuse to be Afraid.
Free yourself. Dream.
• • •
Warren Bluhm

REFUSE TO BE AFRAID

© 2010 Warren Bluhm. All rights reserved. Written and edited by Warren Bluhm. Some of the content of this book was originally posted on the blog "Montag: ... and the clocks were striking thirteen" under the name B.W. Richardson.

This is a September 2021 reproduction of the first edition of *Refuse to be Afraid*.

For more information, visit www.warrenbluhm.com.
ISBN 978-1-7373499-6-9

Carol Jean,
I was afraid I'd never find you.
Thank God I did.

Of waking in the night
to find my life was wasted,
Of thinking as I die
of all the things I've never tasted,
I've been afraid —
But I won't be anymore.

I've been worried if I step outside,
I'll have to take a breath.
I've been worried if I care too much,
someday I'll confront death.
I've been afraid —
But I refuse to be afraid anymore.

A time comes now and then
when it's time to look around,
assess your dreams to see which fly
and which are shattered on the ground.
I've been afraid —
But I won't be anymore.

Everyone who's ever seen the sky
is bound to feel some rain,
and if you never reach that high,
it's just a lonelier kind of pain.
I've been afraid —
But I refuse to be afraid anymore.

All of the days of my life,
I've waited for the night;
All of the ways of my life
I've hidden from the light.
So many times I've yearned to step outside
and couldn't reach the door —
I was afraid,
But I refuse to be afraid anymore.
I need to open that door,
and I won't be afraid anymore.

w.p. bluhm
1992, 1995

Introduction: Refuse to be Afraid

Spend a short time reading, watching and listening, and it soon becomes clear that fear has become the motivating factor in this contemporary world of ours. Life is portrayed as a maelstrom of forces beyond the power of the individual to tame. Terrorists lurk on every street corner seeking to strike fear into our hearts and destroy our way of life. Odd chemicals seeping into the air and water threaten to poison us or raise the temperature of the world to the point where, again, our way of life is threatened.

But the terrifying things aren't all so world-shifting and broad. Gangs roam urban streets and commit violence daily (pay no attention to those reports that suggest violent crime is on the decrease). Chemical additives in our food cause unhealthy and potentially fatal changes in our body chemistry. If you get sick you may not be able to afford your care; thousands already are being denied the treatment they need. The economy is so shaky it could collapse at any moment — or at the very least your employer might be forced to lay you off.

Politicians tap into these fears constantly, instilling in their supporters a fear of the other political party. The other side is not just a collection of people who disagree on the issues; it is a frightening force that threatens our way of life. They present themselves and/or their own political party as the safe and sane solution to the troubles that plague our nation. The solution to these fears is very often a restriction on freedom: After all, the safest place in the world is inside a cage, where no one can reach through the bars to harm you.

The private sector works the same way: Advertisements address a scary thought and then offer you a product that can solve it. Heartburn getting you down? Having trouble sleeping? Having trouble, err, loving? Ask your doctor to prescribe this pill for you.

Or, on a more personal level, the everyday press and stress of making a living conspire to hold us back. We're afraid to follow our dreams and passions because they don't sound as practical as drawing a regular paycheck. And what if our dream project or career does prove to be impractical — now our dream is shattered and we're broke to boot? Or even worse, what if our loved ones don't share our passions and won't help us achieve them? Fear and doubt keep our big ideas in the closet.

We don't even need much help to get scared. We've all heard of the flight-or-fight instinct: When presented with something scary, we either run to safety or — usually if there is no other recourse — stand and fight the menace. This instinct works on such a primal level that we can end up scaring ourselves into submission.

We need to step out in faith, keep going — and refuse to be afraid. My aim here is to help you tame your fear.

The brave man is not he who feels no fear,
For that were stupid and irrational;
But he, whose noble soul its fears subdues,
And bravely dares the danger nature shrinks from.

Joanna Baillie

The cliff

I learned everything I need to know about fear on a steep hill overlooking Lake Champlain in Vermont. I keep coming back to this story whenever anxiety threatens to stop me in my tracks. Childhood lessons sink in deep.

To my younger-than-10-years-old eyes, it looked more like a cliff than a hill; my impression was informed by the shale-like formations that reached down to the beach and disappeared into the pine forest above. Seen from the cabin our parents rented for a week every summer, the forest appeared to grow to the edge of a steep, rocky incline that I wouldn't be able to scale if I had to.

And one day, I had to.

I can still smell the pine trees, I can still feel the soft but prickly bed of needles against my chest, and I still have a dark spot in my heart from the terror as I lost my tenuous grip on the hillside and plunged over the cliff.

Somewhere around 1960 when I was 7, my brothers and I had gone for a walk through the woods near the cabin. Along this stretch the pines clung precariously to the side of the hill.

The pine needles were thick underneath, and I underestimated how unstable the footing would be, as I wandered far down that nearly vertical hillside, trying to peer over the edge to see the beach through the brush. Next thing I knew, I had slipped. The bed of needles was thick, so thick that I couldn't really get a grip, and when I did try to climb, every move I made caused me to slide a little farther down.

I was clinging to the side of the nearly vertical slope and unable to climb upward.

"Go get Dad," I heard my older brother say to my younger brother. "Hang on, War," he called. Hang on to what?

It didn't take long for gravity to do its work, and I slid to the edge and then fell, screaming, over the edge of the embankment to the beach below.

The drop from the edge of the cliff to the beach turned out to be only four, maybe five feet.

When my brothers ran the long way around to the beach, they found me on the ground unharmed, laughing in relief, laughing at myself for being so terrified.

I think about that cliff a lot, when it seems that life has left me hanging by the fingernails. Fear of the unknown makes us scream. Taking on those fears makes us triumphant — perhaps it even makes us giggle uncontrollably.

This is a book about fear, the fear in your heart that makes you want to scream when you're not hanging on to keep from sliding off the side of what you think is a high cliff. It's a book about harnessing the fear long enough to take the plunge. You'll probably find, as I did, that the paralyzing fear of the drop is a whole lot worse than the actual fall.

It's a book that says refuse to be afraid and go ahead and take the leap.

Most things I worry about
never happen anyway.

Tom Petty

The symptoms

I hadn't been alive for very long, and I was pretty sure I didn't want to die yet. The little poster in the front window of the barber shop in Little Falls, N.J., told me it might not be long.

In stark bold letters, the poster announced "The 7 warning signs of leukemia." I didn't know exactly what leukemia was, but it sounded scary and in the late 1950s it was almost always fatal. The poster said it was cancer of the blood.

I did an inventory for the signs. "Change in a mole or wart" — well, my little body was littered with moles, but I was pretty sure they all looked the same as the day before. "Fatigue" — no, I had plenty of energy; I was a kid after all. "Hoarseness" —

I cleared my throat.

Was I hoarse? I did have a little bit of a tickle there, a small frog perhaps. I tried a few words.

"Hello? Hello? Oh no."

My voice was a little ragged.

I might have leukemia! It was a real possibility. The poster said so. My voice was hoarse.

I squirmed my way through the haircut, panic rising in my soul at every clip. Why waste my time with a haircut when I might have so little time to spare?

Afraid to say anything out loud, I was quiet on the way home, and the next time I was with my mother without the brothers around, I approached her and said solemnly, "Mom, I have to talk to you."

She could tell right away that I was a tad distraught. No doubt she looked around the house to see if anything else was broken, but the look on my face told her this was different from guilt. I led her into a bedroom and closed the door.

"What? What is it?" Now she was starting to get anxious herself.

I threw myself against her apron and hung on for dear life.

"One of the symptoms of cancer is hoarseness and *today I'm hoarse!!!*" I wailed.

For just a moment there was no sound in the room except for my terrified sobbing.

And then, a soft laugh.

You know the scene in the movie *A Christmas Story* where Ralphie gets in a fight and afterward his brother, Randy, hides under the kitchen sink? When Mom asks what he's doing there, he screams, "Daddy's gonna kill Ralphie!"

Mom gives a soft chuckle and says reassuringly, "No, Daddy's not going to kill Ralphie."

Every time I see that movie, I laugh out loud because Randy's fear and Mom's reaction are so real. I know, because that's exactly how I sounded that day and exactly how my own mother sounded when she said, "No, you don't have cancer."

Patiently, she told me I needed to have more than one symptom before I needed to consider the most dire diagnosis. I realized I probably was going to live. The fright eased its way out of my tiny frame.

Lesson learned: Wait until you have all of the facts before jumping to conclusions. So often we become afraid because we only understand part of the story. "A little knowledge is a dangerous thing," says the old proverb — but the emphasis is on the word *little*. If you don't have full knowledge, you can make a dangerous mistake: such as being paralyzed by fear.

The leukemia society didn't mean to frighten a little boy that day, but planting a little fear in your mind is a common motivational tactic. The idea of the poster was to get you to a doctor, but it also works for product advertising and politicians.

When I sought more information from the closest trusted source at hand — my mom — the fears were dispelled.

Are you scared of something you don't fully understand? Get more information. Most of the time, the situation is not as dire as you fear. And even more often, as I learned by discovering I didn't have leukemia, the situation is not even a "situation" at all.

'Tis surprising
to see how rapidly
a panic
will sometimes run
through a country.

Thomas Paine

It starts when you're always afraid

No doubt you're afraid of something, or you wouldn't be reading this book.

It's nothing to be ashamed of. I'm scared, too. We all live with fear, ranging from little anxieties to sheer, stark-raving-mad, paralyzing terror, and everything in between. Fear of failure, fear of success, fear of getting started, fear of being stopped before we're finished, fear of what to do next after we're finished. Fear of hate, fear of love, fear of hating, fear of being loved. Fear of sickness, fear of health, fear of other people's habits, fear of our own.

Fear of death.

A portion of this book is necessarily about politics. So many people have found a sure way to get elected is to make voters afraid of something — or someone.

We've come a long way from "the only thing we have to fear is fear itself." Turns out Franklin Roosevelt, who was so wrong about so many things, had that one thing right: Nothing can stop us as dead in the water as cold, stark fear.

From the amount of fear flying through the air on a daily basis, it seems a lot of people have figured out what a great motivator fear can be. Every action our government takes seems to be based on making you afraid and then giving you a false sense of security by tightening your chains. Many businesses thrive on making you afraid of something, then selling you escape or protection.

We are constantly reminded that terrorists would like to do worse things to us than simply fly airliners into crowded buildings — we're told they have suitcase bombs, poison gas and all sorts of other horrors waiting in store for us.

And once we're good and scared, we don't mind having cameras everywhere and screeners feeling us up when we want to enter public places.

After Katrina, we were afraid of hurricanes, but we were told "never fear," because Homeland Security and FEMA were given billions of dollars to shield us from the impact of the next big wind. Storm troopers on every corner in New Orleans made people feel so safe that there was talk of sending in the military to enforce quarantines on the odd chance that avian flu mutates into a strain that affects humans, not just birds.

We're afraid that children will be molested, so we repeal the double-jeopardy law for "sexual predators" and keep them locked up after their prison terms expire. We're afraid of pain, so we put warning labels on everything that could possibly hurt us. We're afraid of cancer, so we verbally abuse anyone who smokes near us and get the city council, the state legislature and anyone who'll listen to ban smoking.

Fear sells, and if paranoia strikes deep enough, fear enslaves. That might not be heartburn, it might be acid reflux disease, but don't worry, here's a pill. Good Lord, what if something terrible happens to you while you're driving? Never fear, we can sell you a cellphone with global positioning capability so people can find you wherever you may stray. What if the next terrorist, the next hurricane, or the next flu bug were to attack you? Never fear, we have troops at the ready to disarm you, oops, that is to say, ready to protect you.

As this book heads to press, the United States is waist-deep in an election campaign. As in all other political campaigns, it seems, the issues are our fears. One side plays on our fear of being unable to make ends meet, of living from paycheck to paycheck, and the terror of what might happen if the paychecks stop coming, of what might happen to our loved ones if anything were to happen to us. Another side plays on our fear of those terrorists, of the people with different faces and/or religions who want to destroy our way of life. Both sides promise that if we will turn responsibility for our personal protection over to them, we will be safe and secure.

Also in the news as this book headed to press, a deep economic downturn was playing on fears in a palpable way. Millions of people were without work, and job security felt like a quaint old notion of days gone by.

It seems like the one constant in life, especially as described by those who want a piece of us: There's always something to be scared of.

There's really only one place where you're totally secure: A jail cell. Surrounded by four walls with barred doors and windows, you can't be hurt. (We'll set aside your fear of earthquakes for the moment.) Government leaders who promise you safety from outside influences can only deliver by caging you – by stripping your liberty away, either one freedom at a time or all at once.

Benjamin Franklin was right, presuming he really said these words attributed to him: "Those who would give up essential liberty to purchase a little temporary safety deserve neither liberty nor safety."

"The only thing we have to fear is fear itself," President Franklin Roosevelt said in his first inaugural address. What does that mean, in the end? It sounds good in a speech, but where was he going with it? Roosevelt himself manipulated fear of economic hard times into a redesign of the U.S. government, creating a taxpayer-financed safety net against another Depression. He trained generations to expect government, not business or individual initiative, to be the engine of the economy, changing the very structure of America.

It was a classic political bait and switch — he told people not to be afraid, then used their fears as a means to his political ends. That's a perfect example of why the only thing we have to fear is indeed fear itself: Fear makes us susceptible to manipulation. Even politicians who urge us not to be afraid may be playing on our fears to forward their agendas.

We must refuse to be afraid, or rather, we must be on guard when we are afraid so that we are not deceived into actions we regret later.

And what is it, in the end that we are afraid of? Ultimately, we are afraid of death. No matter what our "quality of life," to use a well-worn term, we don't want to be not-alive.

We are afraid of dying, but you know what? Everybody does it. Nobody wants to die before "our time," but there are fates worse than death. One such fate is being afraid to live. Another is making security a higher priority than freedom.

You have no guarantee that you'll take another breath, no guarantee that when you woke up this morning you would see the sunset tonight. Don't be afraid of that thought; instead, let it liberate you and motivate you to live as fully as you can – and don't surrender your liberty for a false sense of safety.

The book is called *Refuse to be Afraid*, but you're not human if you're not afraid from time to time. What

I hope to encourage you to do is to keep your fear at bay. Don't let it control your thoughts and actions.

I've been writing about Big Fears, the fears that lead to airport checkpoints and surveillance cameras and sometimes even to wars, but little fears make us miserable, too. We don't speak out for something we believe in, because we're afraid of the repercussions. We don't ask that attractive person for a date, because we're afraid of being turned down. We don't start writing the Great American Novel or quit our jobs and start that business we really want to start – because we're afraid it won't work out. Worse, we're afraid of the changes success will bring in our lives.

When I say, "Refuse to be afraid," I'm not telling you to deny that anxious little feeling or that paralyzing terror. The fear is real. I'm just suggesting that the thing that terrifies you can't possibly be as awful as the paralysis. And yielding control of your life, i.e., your freedom, is likely to produce scarier results than an environment where everyone is free.

Would you rather be safe or free? Too many today would rather be safe, and wily people understand that, tempting us to give up just a little more freedom to be safe.

The New Hampshire license plate says it all: Live free or die. Without freedom, we are the living dead anyway.

We cannot discover new oceans
until we have the courage
to lose sight of the shore.

Muriel Chen

What this book is, and is not

This book does not contain a system, merely an exhortation.

I believe that every human being is an individual, and it is dangerous to group individuals into a collective or make generalizations based on apparent similarities between individuals.

We are snowflakes, not assembly-line products. No two snowflakes are alike, they say, and assembly lines were invented in order to churn out items that are identical in every possible way. Keep in mind, though, that even two products that come off an assembly line are not exactly alike.

What works for me in overcoming fear may not work for you. You may find a ritual or habit that brings your fear under control, but it may prove meaningless to someone else.

I can't tell you how to dissolve your fear. I can merely show you how fear works.

It's good news, actually, that there's no one-size-fits-all fear-killing solution. The reason is that you are a unique individual; no one in the world is quite like you.

Even ideas that have worked for me, most of the time, don't chase the fears away permanently. The trick is to recognize the paralysis — and that's not so hard really. Have you stopped moving forward? You may be paralyzed with fear.

Most important is to find a way to work through the fear, because the paralysis is the worst thing. But it has to be your own way, your own system. Doing it my way won't work.

Author and psychologist Sunni Maravillosa calls it "S.E.S.S." — Someone Else's System Syndrome.

> ... it's alluring to think that we can plug ourselves in to some sequence of steps, and if we follow it accurately, we'll see success. It relieves us of some of the burden of thinking for ourselves or attending to all that's going on: The System has us covered.

But what happens when part of the system becomes problematic, or impossible? Or, despite one's best efforts to follow the system, success doesn't blossom? Most individuals, I suspect, would place the blame on themselves: It's their fault the system doesn't integrate seamlessly into their lives; or there's some hidden failure that keeps success from emerging from the effort put into the system.

I think we tend to overlook this important detail: *it's someone else's system.* It isn't designed for our unique circumstances and idiosyncrasies. And to the degree that one tries to shoehorn oneself into an ill-fitting system, there'll be concomitant difficulties.

... There are no shortcuts or easy outs in life; other people can offer us helpful ideas, but because each of us is in a unique place, with a unique context (our individual combination of history, present situation, and future hopes and goals), any system is best treated as a set of rough suggestions rather than marble steps leading the way to paradise.

What I offer here are thoughts on the nature of fear, and the way it's used to manipulate us, for reasons as innocuous as to sell us acne medicine and as sinister as robbing our freedom. I also offer thoughts about the way we let fears trap ourselves in a place where we'd rather not be — a safe but unfulfilling job, for example.

Many authors have conjured systems and programs to help overcome fears. One or another may work for you, and many may not. I'm not suggesting a one-plan-kills-all-fears approach here, just offering some ways to recognize when you're afraid and help you refuse to succumb to the fear.

But you do need to have a way to deal with being afraid. The main thing to remember is that it can't be somebody else's system.

I think that's why people who want to live a healthier lifestyle have so much trouble sticking to the diet plan or the exercise regimen, for example. They read a book about a certain diet and get all excited, and they try following the directions. When they can't live up to the expectations of somebody else's system, they get discouraged and veer off the routine — and nothing changes. The key is to develop what works for you.

What works for me may not work for you. I can and will give you an idea about how I maintain peace and calm, and if you find some sense there, give it a try. If you still find yourself overcome with self-doubt and anxiety, you need to take a different approach. There are as many ways to face fear down as there are ways to lose weight or improve your cardiovascular health.

But you do need a system — your own system, your own plan of attack for keeping the fear at bay. "If you don't know where you're going, any road will get you there." If you don't know where you going, with no self-reminders when the fear is starting to nag at you and tear you back down, it's easy to get lost and find your way stymied again by fear.

And whatever system you adopt, it must include a recognition of why you're afraid. Knowledge is power.

Look into what holds you back — listen to what your heart is telling you. What are you afraid of? Recognizing the source of the fear is the beginning of overcoming it. You probably will find that your cliff is not nearly as high as you think — it likely is as inconsequential and harmless as my cliff was. And even if it's a tad more formidable than that, you'll still find your darkest fears are not as scary out in the light.

Courage is resistance to fear, mastery of fear — not absence of fear.

Mark Twain

We're all gonna die

My eye was caught at the antique store by a thick, well-worn book titled "Modern Medical Counselor." By its condition it was clear the book was anything but modern, and the price ($2) was right, so, figuring it would be an interesting excursion into the past, I brought it home.

What actually caught my attention was the section that I casually opened to, even before I brought the book home: "Survival in Atomic Bombing." The copyright date of the book is 1951, so browsing through this book will be a traipse through an era where communism and nuclear death were our greatest fears.

With the knowledge of what was to happen in the next 60 years, we know the fears were largely unfounded. Hiroshima and Nagasaki are still the only cities ever destroyed by atomic bombs. Although the great communist bogeyman reared his ugly head many times over the years, the Union of Soviet Socialist Republics fell apart under the weight of its totalitarian follies and China has decided to try burying us the good old American way, by establishing government-subsidized monopolies.

In other words, the fear that was used as an excuse to impose on our liberties never came true. Communism and nuclear catastrophe did not destroy us.

Today, the fear is of small groups of terrorists (and "rogue nations") with nuclear and other weapons of mass destruction. The fear is that an influenza virus that kills birds will find a way to migrate into humans and cause a pandemic. The fear is that standing too close to a person smoking a cigarette will give you cancer. We can let those fears control us, we can let others use those fears to justify locking us into cages, or we can refuse to be afraid and live our lives as free men and women.

Here is the fear that lurks behind all of these fears: We are afraid to die. We are especially afraid to die before we experience a ripe old age.

Here is the truth: We all *will* die, some of us "before our time." The real choice we all have: We can live and die as slaves, or we can live and die as free men and women.

Most of our lives we exist in the gray area between freedom and slavery, convincing ourselves that we are making our choices freely: When we hand the chains to our government and our bosses and our creditors, we rationalize that we are making a free decision to enslave ourselves. And it usually is a freely made choice — in the beginning.

Like Jacob Marley's ghost, we accumulate shackles as we progress through life, usually out of fear — fear of poverty, fear of going hungry, fear of not having a reliable car. And the biggest fear of them all is the fear of death.

Accepting that you will die is the beginning of freedom. The title of the song "Live Like You're Dying" is its message.

These thoughts, especially as I relate them in a political context, could be misconstrued as advocating violent resistance against the slave masters. Nothing could be further from the truth. The revolution I advocate is an internal one:

Refuse to be afraid. Resist the impulse to yield to the fear and let someone strip your liberty in the name of security and protection. Live like you were dying — because you *are* dying, someday, so better to live free than in chains.

The scariest moment
is always just before you start.
After that,
things can only get better.

Stephen King

Procrastination is fear

Some time ago, I devoured the book *48 Days to the Work You Love* and started listening to the weekly podcast of the same name featuring author and career coach Dan Miller.

About midway through one show, Miller addressed the subject of procrastination, which regular visitors know is one of my worst habits.

It was a slap upside the head when he said:

"If you find yourself going weeks and weeks and months and years and never acting, something else is going on. I mean, procrastinating is just another expression of fear, whether it's fear of failure, fear of ridicule of family members and friends, whatever it is that's holding you back ...

"This doesn't have anything to do with circumstances, it doesn't have to do with being too busy. It's a personal issue. You can break that logjam and move into things that really are meaningful."

Procrastinating is just another expression of fear. Hard words to hear for a guy who was several years into writing a book on the subject "Refuse to be afraid." But he was right!

The question then becomes: What are procrastinators afraid of?

A dear friend of mine went into the hospital 20-odd years ago for open heart surgery. It was a risky proposition at the time, and she made all the necessary preparations just in case: Funeral arrangements, a will, arrangements for her pets to be adopted by friends.

Then she survived the surgery with flying colors. I remember seeing a confused expression in her eyes as her friends surrounded her hospital bed with cheer.

The reason for the confusion became apparent as years went by and her life drifted without direction. She had tied her life up in a tidy ball and prepared to die, you see.

But she had given no thought and made no preparations to live.

I think procrastination might be a fear of living. You have made no plan and considered no purpose, as my friend did, or else you have the plan and you're afraid to execute it. Fear of failure? That seems logical — no one wants to pursue a dream and lose everything that is tangible. I think fear of success is a real thing, too — look how miserable are so many people who have achieved the image of success. For one thing, they've lost their privacy: That's how we can see how miserable they are.

If you're procrastinating, resolve today to take one step towards the dream. Just one will do; for me it was taking an extra 15 minutes to finish this chapter before pushing myself away from the keyboard. Breaking the chains of procrastination fear is as simple and as complicated as overcoming inertia, which is accomplished merely by a sufficient push: Just get started.

The whole aim of practical politics is
to keep the populace alarmed
(and hence clamorous to be led to safety)
by menacing it with an endless series of hobgoblins,
most of them imaginary.

H.L. Mencken

The politics of fear

Towards the climax of the great dystopian movie about violence and the state *V for Vendetta*, megalomaniacal leader Adam Sutler declares the time has come for the rulers of totalitarian England to remind the peasantry "why they need us." What follows is a montage of news reports clearly intended to cow the citizenry into a state of fear, reminding them that the government is the only thing standing between their security and utter chaos.

According to the litany of bad news, a civil war drags on in the former United States. Water shortages are reported and predicted because of a lack of sufficient rain for two years. Police arrest nine suspects who were hoarding vaccine against the deadly avian flu. Twenty-seven people have died in the wake of the discovery of a new airborne disease. New evidence links the terrorist V to an attack on London 14 years earlier — reminding them of the attack that made citizens turn to the government for protection in the first place.

A skeptical bar patron says out loud: "Can you believe this shit?" Of course we can't, and we shouldn't.

The truth revealed by the movie is that the state led by Sutler is the source of the chaos. The titular character V, either a freedom fighter or a terrorist depending upon point of view, helps detective Finch uncover the reality that the central terrorist attack of his age was staged by government forces seeking control of citizens' lives under the cover of providing more security. V himself is the product of secret government medical research gone awry.

A central theme of the movie is the same as mine: Refuse to be afraid. The standard political script has been unchanged for decades now: Remind people about something they fear. Offer yourself as the solution to that which they fear. Once elected, strip people of freedom in the name of fighting that which they fear. Rule with an iron fist or a velvet glove, but rule; do not let people live for themselves in freedom.

I would like to dig one notch deeper: V himself preys upon fear, as well. He manipulates people's fear of the state and their fear of losing their freedom — a healthy fear, no doubt, but a real and palpable fear. Notice that V's agenda is first vengeance against the people who conducted the secret medical research on him — hence the title *V for Vendetta.* He justifies his vendetta by wrapping it within the more worthy cause of freedom: "People should not be afraid of their governments; governments should be afraid of their people." But this little proverb betrays his agenda: It explicitly expresses a belief that *someone should be afraid*.

Fear is the great irrationalizer. People do stupid and terrible things when they are afraid. Therefore governments, comprised of people acting as a collective, do stupid and terrible things when they operate out of fear. It is one thing to be aware of danger; it is entirely a different thing to be so afraid of that danger that you do or allow stupid and terrible things.

Being aware of the state's incomprehensible assault on our freedom is a healthy thing. Allowing yourself to become afraid of the state, and acting based on that fear rather than rational awareness, is unhealthy.

The state wants you to be afraid. Refuse to be afraid of their straw men and speculations. When the news raises that little bug in your stomach that tells you you're getting scared, take note and think: Who benefits from my fear, and why? Often a politician will offer a proposal to alleviate your fear, but it will involve giving up a bit of liberty in exchange. What is that politician's real agenda? You may — you probably will — find that you are being menaced with one of Mencken's imaginary hobgoblins. Don't let a manipulative statesman get you clamoring to be led to safety. That way, eventually, lies tyranny.

But go one step beyond: Refuse to be afraid of the state itself. When folks like me show you examples of the state's fear-mongering, use the information to think for yourself.

Don't be afraid of the state's power, because fear is part of the fuel of their power. We do not need the state to take care of us; the real truth is about how much our leaders need us to believe we need them.

It's not only politicians who have an agenda, however. If criticism of the state results in your being paralyzed by fear of the state, you may be being manipulated in another direction. It's vital to ask, "Why am I afraid?"

And that brings us to the second part of this book's mantra: Free yourself.

The character Evie is unable to think clearly until she has no more fear. She reaches that condition of bliss only after a lifetime of horror and several weeks of torture — not a regimen any of us would like to undergo. Perhaps the best we can do is acknowledge our fears and refuse to allow the fear to control our actions and decisions. But that is the key — defeating the fear and living free.

Tired of lugging all those chains around? Take a second look and see how many of the shackles are of your own making. And of the shackles you forged for yourself, how many of them are imaginary? Sometimes, when you're convinced you're up against a brick wall, the solution is to try walking through the wall to see if it's really there.

Always — Always! — when the news of the day causes you to grow anxious and afraid for your future or your children's future, look around: Who is it who benefits from your fear? How do the "practical politicians" propose to solve the crisis caused by the latest menacing hobgoblin — and how do The Powers That Be profit by passing this legislation (it's always legislation)?

Resist any solution that steals more freedom or independence from you or your business or your property. Ask why. "Why is this hobgoblin such a menace that the only solution you propose is to restrict our freedom and take our liberty away?"

Shine a light and the rodents may scurry away — even if they don't, the things they tell you to fear won't seem nearly as big and terrifying shining in the sun as they do now, hiding in the midnight darkness.

Refuse to be afraid. It's hardest to keep your fears under control when so many forces are trying so hard to alarm you. No doubt they have fearful purposes of their own, but they feed on our fear. Refuse to be afraid. It's the first step on beyond the paralysis of fear, the first step toward freeing yourself and following your dreams.

Living in fear is an oxymoron.

Leonard Pitts Jr.

Gojira and the cuddly monster syndrome: Laugh away your fear

From time to time I wonder about the process that converted Godzilla into the star of a series of movies that appeal mostly to children.

The 1954 Japanese film *Gojira* is a remarkable drama. Nine years after the atomic destruction of Hiroshima and Nagasaki, a prehistoric creature emerges from the depths of the seas, shaken loose by the vibrations of nuclear bomb testing and mutated to unnatural proportions by the bombs' radiation.

A scientist has created a weapon even more terrible than an atomic bomb, one so horrible that he refuses to share the process he used to discover the technology and resists efforts to use the weapon against the giant creature, even as Japan's largest city comes under siege. Thousands die and Tokyo is largely demolished before the scientist agrees to unleash the weapon, but he does it in a way that claims his own life. He has already destroyed his notes, so he has ensured that the ugly weapon dies with him.

It's a movie about war, peace, violence and nonviolence, technology and the simple ongoing question: Just because something *can* be done, is it right and just to do it? A very thoughtful and important movie with fantasy and science fiction elements.

Gojira was repackaged as *Godzilla, King of the Monsters*, for distribution in America, and each and every one of its more than 20 sequels has been mindless child's play. One almost has to wonder: What was so dangerous about the ideas in *Gojira* that it had to be so trivialized?

But maybe the devolution of Godzilla was only natural. After all, scary monsters are often transformed into cuddly children's toys. Look at the stark and poignant story of the man built from parts of other men by Dr. Frankenstein. The iconic image of

Boris Karloff in his monster makeup eventually became Herman Munster.

Perhaps it's simply a natural reaction to looking into the depths of the soul and finding darkness. We step away, we dress up the darkness with childlike innocence, and we look the other way. A person can only spend so much in the dark before needing a little sunshine.

There's a technique for coping with fear here: Laugh at it. Think of the object of your fear transformed into something cuddly. It's easier to wrap your arms and mind around a sweet, soft teddy bear than a hungry grizzly. Once again, our nastiest fears seldom come true. Almost every airplane ride ends with a safe landing. Most of the time a sharp headache is caused by something other than a brain tumor. Visualize the worst that can happen, then realize it's not going to happen (and if it does, you can cope with it) — and as I did at the bottom of that fearsome Vermont cliff, you may discover yourself laughing at your fear.

Conspiracy to suppress dangerous ideas didn't necessarily turn Gojira into Godzilla, or Frankenstein's monster into a comedic cliché. It could be simply that we needed to be reassured that, sometimes, things that go bump in the night are just bumps.

For God
has not given us
a spirit of fear,
but of power and of love
and of a sound mind.

2 Timothy 1:7
New King James Version

Jesus

I have always taken some comfort from several passages in the Gospel of Matthew, especially (for purposes of this discussion especially) the reassurance not to worry. It's part of Jesus' oft-quoted Sermon on the Mount, and in its context provides some attitude adjustments that have aided me in my own struggle with doubts and fears.

As a Christian my own path to refusing to be afraid inevitably works its way through Matthew 6: 17-34.

> Do not store up for yourselves treasures on Earth, where moth and rust destroy, and where thieves break in and steal. But store up for yourselves treasures in heaven, where moth and rust do not destroy, and where thieves do not break in and steal.

For where your treasure is, there your heart will be also.

The eye is the lamp of the body. If your eyes are good, your whole body will be full of light. But if your eyes are bad, your whole body will be full of darkness. If then the light within you is darkness, how great is that darkness!

No one can serve two masters. Either he will hate the one and love the other, or he will be devoted to the one and despise the other. You cannot serve both God and Money.

Therefore I tell you, do not worry about your life, what you will eat or drink; or about your body, what you will wear. Is not life more important than food, and the body more important than clothes?

Look at the birds of the air; they do not sow or reap or store away in barns, and yet your heavenly Father feeds them. Are you not much more valuable than they? Who of you by worrying can add a single hour to his life?

And why do you worry about clothes? See how the lilies of the field grow. They do not labor or spin. Yet I tell you that not even Solomon in all his splendor was dressed like one of these.

If that is how God clothes the grass of the field, which is here today and tomorrow is thrown into the fire, will he not much more clothe you, O you of little faith?

So do not worry, saying, 'What shall we eat?' or 'What shall we drink?' or 'What shall we wear?' For the pagans run after all these things, and your heavenly Father knows that you need them.

But seek first his kingdom and his righteousness, and all these things will be given to you as well.
Therefore do not worry about tomorrow, for tomorrow will worry about itself. Each day has enough trouble of its own.

The three lines that I boldfaced pretty much sum up what I believe as a Christian — that the more I align my life with the One who created this life and this universe, the more peace I feel and the easier it is to keep my fear under control.

I have always gotten in trouble when I put my love of Stuff over the more important things in life, like loved ones or health or making the world a better place — and make no mistake, Stuff is Money. Stuff is what Jesus was writing about when he warned about making Money your master.

When fear gets its grip on me, it's usually because I've lost alignment with the Power of the universe. That spirit of power and love is a calming spirit that clears the mind and cleanses fear away.

Yes, some practitioners of Christianity dwell on fear — my goodness, one of the most famous sermons in history is still Jonathan Edwards' 1741 composition "Sinners in the Hands of an Angry God," with its ruminations on what happens to sinners who fail to accept Christ in their lives. There's not much scarier than the prospect of eternal damnation.

But a true life in Christ is not about fear. Jesus said it all comes down to two basic commands: Love God, and love one another. Living in harmony with the creator of the universe and with each other is a pretty solid way to live without fear, I'd say.

I know, I told you this book is not about getting you to buy into "somebody else's system." But I'd be remiss if I didn't share some of what works for me. Feel free to delve further into the question of who Jesus is, or ignore it. You will have to find your own path to peace.

The greatest mistake you can make in life
is to be continually fearing
you will make one.

Elbert Hubbard

Friends don't let friends drown in the quotidian

Fear gives us a million excuses not to free ourselves from the quotidian. I know what you're thinking: What the heck is the quotidian?

An interesting exchange — and a new word for me — occurred after I wrote an online book report about Ayn Rand's *The Fountainhead*. It's about a principled architect who won't compromise his attitude to accept nothing short of excellence from himself. I wrote about how the book had filled me with motivation to do my best and exercise my creative juices.

A short while after I posted the review on my blog, a commenter named CK wrote: "So many had that same feeling you have expressed after reading *The Fountainhead* or *Atlas Shrugged;* don't be alarmed, the feeling will pass."

I responded, "CK, I hope when you said 'the feeling will pass' you didn't mean the feeling where I said 'It makes me want to go write another Great American Novel, compose a symphony or two, and otherwise exercise my muse to death.'"

"That is exactly what I meant," CK replied. "The quotidian wins over the exalted.

"In *Fountainhead*, Rand created archetypes; in *Atlas Shrugged* she fleshed them out. Finish *A.S.* and you will know the exaltation feeling again and a few weeks or months or years later and you reread *A.S.* and wonder what happened to you in the interim. The symphony will not be finished, the Great Novel or Expose will remain inchoate; the world-shaking business plan will have gathered dust in the face of the inevitable quotidian."

Quotidian: adj. (rhet.), daily, occurring every day.

What a great word! What a depressing observation! And perhaps/probably true. From the launch of my blog, I had been occasionally writing about my hopes and dreams for the future, things I'm going to do someday when I break away from the, err, quotidian. And sure enough, the daily grind, the wage-slave job, kept getting in the way.

Eight days after finishing *The Fountainhead* with that incredible exhilaration, I had tinkered around the edges of the dreams, set down a page full of notes about the novel, worked on a number of side projects — and worked the day job as usual, caught Sunday's ball game, a couple of my favorite TV shows. I don't think CK was trying to throw cold water as much as keep me grounded in reality, but I must say that without his/her little tweak, I may not even have done that small amount of tinkering around the edges.

That's the challenge of motivational moments — staying motivated. What I needed was to capture the fire in the belly that comes when you've lost your wage-slave job and have to find a new way to keep the lights on and put food on the table — and do it while maintaining the wage-slave job as a security blanket. Is that wanting to have my cake and eat it, too? Not exactly.

CK came under some criticism from other commentators. But from the beginning, I saw this person as someone who was on my side, who warned me that my burst of creative inspiration upon finishing *The Fountainhead* would probably be beaten down by the quotidian — which, after consulting my dictionary, I interpreted as a friendly reminder that the day-to-day drudgery of earning a living in the Job Culture would tug unceasingly at my desires.

It was a more-than-gentle splash of hard reality, but I took it as helpful advice — better to hear it from a friendly voice in advance than to be surprised by it later on.

Or, to affirm that I understood the original intention, as CK wrote in response to my musing: "I was not intending to throw cold water or subtly shiv your aspirations; I was just giving a warning of what to expect when you actually go for it and start to succeed."

And, in that context, it was a successful warning!

That rascally quotidian had indeed gummed up the works, and the New Novel — let alone this book you're reading today — was not much further along than it was when I first wrote about it a couple of weeks earlier.

But on the plus side, my thoughts had been refined and clarified and my confidence rebuilt to the point where I feel compelled to add this warning for you now: If I succeed with this book, you will set it down with a sense of empowerment and a commitment that you will refuse to be afraid, you will take steps to free yourself, and you will start dreaming of ways to improve your life. And after a very short while, the realities of everyday life will start to tug at your fearlessness. You'll start having doubts and fears again, and the job or other daily tasks will sidetrack your dreaming ability.

That's the dreaded quotidian doing its nasty work again. You have two basic choices: Fall back into the daily drudgery again, or shake it off, stay focused and keep refusing to be afraid.

It'll happen. I hate to tell you, but it's true. The good news is: You've been warned. Be alert to the symptoms of sinking and pull yourself back up to the surface.

Don't let yourself drown in the quotidian.

You'll break the worry habit
the day you decide
you can meet and master
the worst that can happen to you.

Arnold Glasgow

Would you rather be safe or free?

It's been the central question in the United States of America for more than a decade now.

In April 1999 a couple of kids at Columbine High School in Littleton, Colo., committed an atrocity, shooting 35 students and teachers, killing 13 of them, before turning the guns on themselves. In the days immediately after, there was much talk about clamping down on the possession of guns and adding great layers of security to the classroom experience.

I wrote this in my newspaper column in the aftermath:

Would you rather be safe or free?

Those are the choices, you know. There are ways you can try to protect yourself and your children from the possibility that the events of Littleton, Colo., never again happen. But the only way to do it is to lock us all in cages.

You can have a society where no one tells you what church to attend, where no one monitors what you read, write or say, where no one keeps you from going to a Packers game or driving to see an old friend in Missouri.

But you run the risk that someone else may worship Satan or Hitler, that someone may read, write or say persuasively hateful things, that someone at the Packer game may try to sell you a $40 ticket for $250, that bad people will use the Interstate to transport illegal goods or kidnap your daughter.

So the solution is to regulate what church you can go to, what you read and write and say, and place checkpoints at city limits and state borders.

You can have a society where you are free to protect your property or defend your person, or to hunt and feed your family.

But you run the risk that someone with a sick mind will arm himself and kill you or your children.

So the solution is to make sure only the police and military have weapons.

You can have a society where, if you obey the law, no police officer or military unit will ever knock on your door and search through your personal belongings or drag you down to the county jail.

But you run the risk that your next-door neighbor is manufacturing narcotics in his basement or scheming to overthrow the government.

So the solution is a police state.

You can have a society where, if you are accused of a crime, no one can throw you in jail without proof, or torture a confession out of you, or force you to testify under oath that you did it — even if you did it.

But you run the risk that murderers will occasionally escape justice, or criminals get out of prison and commit new crimes.

So the solution is to lock us all up.

When you have a free society, there will be times when someone abuses his or her freedom and harms someone else, perhaps even kills someone else.

The only way to try to prevent such abuses is to take away our freedoms.

And the bad things will not go away.

Confiscate our guns, and criminals will use knives or bombs made of pipe or fertilizer — or steal guns — and we will be defenseless.

Regulate what the media reports, and you lose the right to know what's happening. Regulate the Internet and you depend on the government to inform you. Regulate what singers can sing, writers can write, and painters can paint, and you begin to lose life itself.

And even then, you will not be safe. You will only have built a cage and crawled in. It will be easier for evil to find you when it decides to look.

So how to prevent future school shootings?

Teach children right from wrong. Teach them to cherish life and other living things. Teach them good choices from bad. And punish them when they do wrong, when they harm living things, when they choose badly.

Our nation, this bold experiment, has thrived because of the notion that the only limit on my freedom is that it not impose on yours. The most defining speech of our history concludes, "Give me liberty or give me death!"

Sometimes the people of the world look at America and says, "How can they tolerate such things!" But most of the time they envy America and wish to live in a society as tolerant as ours. Immigration has always outpaced emigration because of our promise.

We must live free. Or we die.

* * * * *

Two years and five months later, 9/11 happened. This time the calls for greater security went far beyond the schoolhouse doors, and I found myself revisiting this theme. The fear in the air was palpable, but so was the anger and the desire to do something — anything — to make sure it never happened again.

It took me more than a week to overcome my own fear this time, the fear that readers would choose safety over freedom. I had already been raked over a few coals for questioning the wisdom of passing the USAPATRIOT Act while emotions were still running high, so I wasn't sure how readers would react to these thoughts. In late October 2001, I decided I'd refuse to be afraid, and I wrote:

The question, "Would you rather be safe or free?" is more relevant today than ever before.

We can be as safe as humanly possible if we are willing to give up our freedom and privacy. Just let security personnel pry into your bag, your car trunk, pat you down, monitor your telephone calls and your mail and your e-mail, track your purchases and the company you keep and the books you read and the TV shows you watch, and keep a camera on you 24 hours a day, and you will probably be safe from harm.

In Ray Bradbury's most famous work, *Fahrenheit 451*, about a dreary world where it is illegal to own books or you and they will be burned, he even notes that people voluntarily relinquish their freedom for the comfort of safety, or in the context of the book, happiness.

The idea was that books exposed you to contrary beliefs that hurt people.

"It didn't come from the government down," a character explains. "There was no dictum, no declaration, no censorship to start with, no! Technology, mass exploitation and minority pressure carried the trick … Today, thanks to them, you can stay happy all the time …"

The common consensus is that on Sept. 11, the question became more than hypothetical. We have sent soldiers abroad to protect our freedom while launching a debate about how far to restrict our freedom to keep America safe.

And for the most part, people are cheerfully surrendering their liberty. When Russ Feingold, D-Wis., was the only senator who said, in effect, "Wait a minute, this antiterrorism bill might be used to harm freedom of innocent people at home, I can't vote for this," it was everyday citizens, not the government, who cried out against him.

When this writer wrote a couple of lines praising Feingold for that vote, it was not the government who took us to task, it was a local radio personality, who added, "Maybe they want to get one of those anthrax letters over there."

On Oct. 8, 2001, Larry Ellison, founder and chief executive officer of Oracle Corp., wrote a column in the Wall Street Journal arguing that the time may have come to issue everyone a national ID card.

"On the face of it, issuing ID cards does seem a significant step," Ellison wrote. "Trusting government to maintain a database with our names, addresses, places of work, amounts and sources of income, assets, purchases, travel destinations, and more, seems a huge leap of faith.

"But we should remember that these databases already exist, and that we willingly helped in their creation."

He goes on to say that by creating a huge, credit-card style, government database to track each of us — and Oracle has "generously" offered to give the government the necessary software for free — we can ensure our safety.

"Only by giving our intelligence and law enforcement agencies better tools can we expect to save life and liberty together," Ellison said.

Save life, yes. Liberty? Well, would you rather be safe or free? The database could alert the police that you checked the Quran and the Unabomber's book out of the library. Does that make you a suspect or someone who wants to understand your enemy?

Forget the ID card — the technology now exists to implant a microchip in a person. Perhaps we would all be safer if we "forced everyone, small and great, rich and poor, free and slave, to receive a mark on his right hand or on his forehead, so that no one could buy or sell unless he has the mark."

Ellison is said to have pitched his idea to Attorney General John Ashcroft, a devout Pentecostal who surely has read the book of Revelation often enough to know when he is on the wrong side.

The House of Representatives wisely added a five-year expiration date to the brave new police powers in the antiterrorism bill, to give us all a chance to review how well they have worked.

It's a trick question — we can be safe *and* free, if the authorities are required to give us back our liberty after the danger has passed. Do you think they'll be willing to give it back?

*****

A few more years have gone by, and more than one senator have now questioned the wisdom behind that antiterrorism law, but we're still waiting to get those freedoms back. Fear can be that powerful.

Do the thing you fear,
and the death of fear
is certain.

Ralph Waldo Emerson

You are where you are

It's not at all unusual for people to have a sense of dissatisfaction about their circumstances. "I really don't have a peace that I'm where God wants me to be." Or: "This is not where I envisioned being at this stage in my life." Or worse: "I don't know what I want to do with my life, but I know it's not this."

I think the question to ask is: What can you do where you are, while you're there?

A small bit that is good news and bad news: Probably every life ends with something left unfinished. If you're living life to the fullest, you'll always be working on something until you can't anymore. So if you have a nagging feeling or a firm conviction that your life's mission is something else, don't fret too much about it, just start working on getting to that something (or somewhere) else. And if you're not too sure what your purpose is, well, start thinking (and, if you're so inclined, praying) — with a little self-examination, you'll find that mission, or you may discover you're already doing it.

And for better or for worse, you are where you are now. See what's possible under these circumstances because, for the moment, this is what you have to work with.

What I'm saying is more than the old cliché "Bloom where you're planted." You have a huge advantage over a plant: You're mobile. You don't stay planted. You're on a journey. Not only are you not required to stay in one place, that's completely opposite of who and what you are.

To a huge extent the journey is the reward. The downside is if you don't know where you're going, any road will get you there. OK, those are both clichés, but they're better clichés and more to the point than "Bloom where you're planted."

And even more to the point, you won't make any progress if you spend too much time moping about being at this particular spot on your journey. Much is made in Christian theology about how Jesus worked with people where they were — he mingled with people his society despised, even (gasp!) tax collectors. If he worked miracles with those folks in their circumstances, he can work miracles with you in yours.

You are where you are. What can you accomplish while you're there? And if you're dissatisfied with where you are, what can you do — now — to get where you'd rather be? There's enough time in every day to do what you're doing and work on the things that will get you elsewhere, even if you can only find time for just one tiny step.

If you're sure you want to be somewhere else, taking those steps will make you feel better. And even if you're not sure, taking steps in one direction will help you clarify if it is, indeed, the direction you want to go. Sometimes exploration reveals you already are where you were "meant" to be. More likely the uneasiness is a signal to get moving.

But you are where you are. This is what you have to work with. "What next?" is a decent question. A better question: What now?

Do not anticipate trouble,
Or worry about
What may never happen.
Keep in the sunlight.

Benjamin Franklin

Dream: You cannot fail

"Self-help" is an entire category of book; an industry has grown around materials that give people advice about how to live a more successful life. I think the reason more people don't find success is that they spend more time studying the principles than putting the principles into action.

One question I find frequently in such materials is: What would you do today, right here and right now, if you knew you could not fail? A corollary of the question: What would you do today, right here and right now, if money was no object?

The point of posing these questions is to remove obstacles to your thinking process. Too often creativity is held back by fear of failure or by the perception that a great deal of money is required to launch whatever endeavor you may be considering.

Therefore it's a liberating and exciting exercise to set your mind free by imagining you can't fail and/or that you can afford everything you need to succeed. But one more step is necessary to pop your dream over the top and into reality.

Imagine this: You're not imagining things.

You *cannot* fail. Money *is* no object.

I need you to ponder that carefully, I need that to sink in, so I'm going to repeat it.

You cannot fail. Money is no object.

When you set your mind on a vision that fires up your dreams, it's as if the forces of the universe align to make it happen. Try not to think too hard about why that's true, but understand it is true.

It's popular to refer to this as The Law of Attraction. Books have been written about it, most recently and famously *The Secret*. which brings to a modern audience the concepts Wallace Wattles described in *The Science of Getting Rich*. I am not sure I buy the idea that a creative universal stuff exists to form the future into what we will, but I do agree with Wattles that we are born to be creative, not competitors, and there's plenty of stuff for everyone.

And I do know that you can accomplish anything you set your mind to. How and why that happens is not necessarily important. Maybe it's simply that people sense your enthusiasm and are drawn to help. Maybe it's that catching the fire of your inner passion generates an energy that makes you do what's necessary. Maybe God rewards the fact that your passion and energy finally align with how He designed you; yep, that's how I envision it, but if you have issues with the idea of supernatural power, don't dwell on it. The important thing is overcoming the illusion that you might fail.

Just know that dreams are contagious. When you set your mind on a vision that fires up your dreams, something makes it begin to happen. Understanding that you cannot fail ignites the dreams.

James Allen explained it best in his motivational classic *As A Man Thinketh*: "All that a man achieves and all that he fails to achieve is the direct result of his own thoughts. In a justly ordered universe, where loss of equipoise would mean total destruction, individual responsibility must be absolute. A man's weakness and strength, purity and impurity, are his own, and not another man's; they are brought about by himself, and not by another; and they can only be altered by himself, never by another. His condition is also his own, and not another man's. His suffering and his happiness are evolved from within. As he thinks, so he is; as he continues to think, so he remains."

Allen set forth a truth that Henry Ford stated even more succinctly: Whether you think you'll succeed or you think you'll fail, you're right.

Most people — if they even bother to go through the exercise and answer a question like "What would you do if you knew you could not fail?" — feel a burst of creative energy, get in touch with their dreams and inner passion, and then step back and think, "Well, that was an interesting exercise. Too bad for all the reasons why I can't do that stuff."

The people who succeed find a way to stay in touch with that inner passion. They discover that it wasn't just a mental exercise.

What would you do today, right now and right here, if you knew you could not fail? Hang onto that thought, because here comes the kicker: It's true. Refuse to be afraid, free yourself and hang onto your dream, and you cannot fail. So you may as well get started.

Faith comes naturally
to people;
that's why we dream.

Mark Gungor

Free yourself. Dream. Rinse; repeat

Still scared? Alarmed? Wondering what to do next?

Join the crowd. It's all a little overwhelming if you let it.

If. You. Let. It.

Fear is a choice. When I write "refuse to be afraid," I'm not trying to tell you to ignore or deny the existence of the little heebie-jeebies that plague your mind, your heart and your gut. It's more an exhortation to keep moving despite them.

Twain got it right — Courage is acknowledging the paralyzing potential of fear and stepping forward anyway. 'Don't be afraid" is in some ways a silly thing to say. We *are* afraid. Life is scary. Accept it, digest it, confront it, and refuse to let it dominate you. Free yourself from the fear, and you can start to dream.

Refuse to be afraid. Free yourself. Dream.

Rinse. Repeat.

I've found the three-step exhortation I evolved for this book's title and subtitle has multiple applications. I started saying "Refuse to be afraid" because so much of modern communication seems to be about raising fears. Terrorists are lurking in every dark corner of the land, most of the food you eat may give you cancer or make you obese or both, and termites may eat the foundation of your house unless you treat it with a certain product.

My advice was simply not to fall for it. Refuse to be afraid. OK, you're nervous and/or scared, but don't let it control you. Refuse to be controlled by your fear.

Then I realized not being afraid was only the first step. You're not afraid, fine. Now what? "Free yourself." Get loose from the chains of your fear. Resist the solutions offered by the politicians and the salesmen and create your own answers. Fly.

But free yourself to do what? Fly where? That's where the dreaming starts.

Releasing the fear makes you free — free to dream — dream of doing something amazing.

It's more than about politics and government, of course. Our fears keep us from taking steps to improve our lives and/or the lives of others — we are held back in our personal lives, our careers by often irrational fears. Others may have instilled a spirit of being afraid in us, but we own that fear and we each have the power to overcome it.

It seems to me the process is the same in most cases:

1. Refuse to be afraid.
2. Now that your fear is under control, you can free yourself to consider many options or take the action you feared.
3. Once free, you can set goals, objectives, dreams ... and go for it! (Whatever "it" may be.)

And then move on to the next fear ... rinse, repeat.

There's a reason a cliché's a cliché: A cliché is a truth that is told repeatedly until the meaning is almost lost. A saying dubbed The Serenity Prayer is one such truth — that the key is to find the courage to change the things I have the power to change, the serenity to accept the things I can't, and the wisdom to know the difference.

Perhaps in the Serenity Prayer lie the answers to maintaining one's sanity — and to refusing to be afraid so that you are free to dream.

Free yourself. Dream. Rinse; repeat.

It's the failures of this world that you turn around and build to make success.
It's the broken dreams that force you to be more when you can settle for less.
It's the wanting to live forever that leads you to a goal that will not die.
It's the wanting to see the stars that gives a simple soul the will to fly.

Warren Bluhm

Final word: A simple truth

A funny thing happened to me on my way toward producing a book called *Refuse to be Afraid*, designed to help people overcome the everyday and extraordinary fears that stand in the way of their freedom and their dreams.

I got scared.

What if everyone already knows this stuff and I'm the last to figure it out? What if I help everyone overcome their fears and it turns out it was good to be afraid — after all, just because you're paranoid doesn't mean someone isn't really out to get you? What if I'm just writing a collection of clichés that no one can take seriously? What if — What if — ?

It took two or three extra years for me to finish this book, because I didn't follow the advice I was laying out in this book. So I bring you these suggestions from personal experience and to say: I know how you feel. I've been there. And there's a way through this.

I've been there — stuck at the beginning of my big project. Lost and confused midway on the path to fulfilling my dreams. Before I could share the advice in this book, I first had to start believing it myself.

Oh, and one other thing. Many of the thoughts in this book began as blog entries I wrote using the name B.W. Richardson. B.W., of course, is my initials reversed, and my father's name is Richard, so the pseudonym came easily.

I started blogging as B.W. in part because I was afraid to use my real name, for reasons that no longer seem relevant. You see my problem, of course. Who wants to read a book called Refuse to be Afraid by a guy who fears the consequences of using his "real" name? B.W. does feel "real" to me in a sense, but for this book to mean anything, he had to go — or at least he had to come out into the light.

So why should you read a book about not being afraid from someone who let fear delay this project not for weeks or months but years?

Because we both know I'm not alone. Because I know some people never pursue their dreams. Because the manipulators will always try to use our universal fears to control us. Because clever marketers and wily politicians will always be willing to tap those fears for their own purposes.

Because I found my way out of that mess — and so can you.

The evidence that my fears were ungrounded is right here: You're reading the book I was afraid would be ignored and dismissed, the thoughts that I was afraid to share under my own name.

You can get past your fears, too. It gets easier with every step you take — but make no mistake, the fear will never completely go away.

So: you're scared. So am I — some days more than others. The first step was recognizing that almost all of the time, I was afraid of nothing. I learned that fear is an irrational and useless emotion. It is a seductive and dangerous force that urges us to stay in our comfort zones: Anything more than the quotidian, the familiar, is scary — sometimes a little scary, sometimes downright frightening.

But you were made for more than this. Refuse to be afraid. Free yourself. Dream. And you will succeed.

Warren Bluhm
September 2010

About the author

Warren Bluhm is an award-winning writer and editor who lives not far from the shores of Green Bay with his best friend, Carol Jean, and an assortment of furry companions. He shares his birthday with the Door County Advocate and has found his greatest professional contentment to date in the stewardship of that venerable community newspaper.

Find books written and edited by Warren Bluhm, along with new essays, music, podcasts and more, at **www.warrenbluhm.com**.

www.ingramcontent.com/pod-product-compliance
Lightning Source LLC
Chambersburg PA
CBHW020912080526
44589CB00011B/562